Alpha Delta Phi Union Chapter

Songs of the Alpha Delta Phi

Alpha Delta Phi Union Chapter

Songs of the Alpha Delta Phi

ISBN/EAN: 9783337090142

Printed in Europe, USA, Canada, Australia, Japan

Cover: Foto ©Thomas Meinert / pixelio.de

More available books at **www.hansebooks.com**

SONGS

OF

ALPHA DELTA PHI.

Published by the Union Chapter in the Thirty-Third year of
the Fraternity.

ALBANY, MDCCCLXIV.

SONGS OF ALPHA DELTA PHI.

I.

ΧΑΙ͂ΡΕ, ᾺΛΦΑ ΔΈΛΤΑ ΦΙ͂!

AIR — "Lauriger Horatius."

Χαῖρε, Ἄλφα Δέλτα Φῖ!
Ἐις αἰῶνα θάλλων,
Ἄυξάνοιο δυνάμει,
Καθ' ἅπαντα νικῶν.

Σελήνη τικτομένη,
Ἄστρον καὶ μαρμαίρον ·
Μέλψομεν εὐφροσύνῃ,
Ὑμῖν ἀσμα φαιδρόν.

Ἐνθάδε Καλλιόπη,
Σὺν πάσαις Μονσάων,
Ναίεται ἐν συναφῇ,
Ἡμᾶς πράως τρέφων.
        Σελήνη τικ-ομένη, κ. τ. λ.

Ναὸς Καλοῦ κ'Ἀγαθοῦ!
Ἐις αἰῶνα στήσων,
Ἐράωμεν σοῦ ἱροῦ,
Ἐράωμεν κυδῶν.
        Σελήνη τικτομέμη, κ. τ. λ.

GEO. S. BISHOP, Amherst.

II.

CARMEN SALUTATIONIS.

Air—" *Gaudeamus Igitur.*"

Veniatis, Socii,
Fugiat tempestas, } *Bis.*
In sermone lepido,
In canore consono,
Nunc agamus horas. *Bis.*

Via nostra dulcis est,
Flosculis ornata; } *Bis.*
Stellâ lucidissimâ,
Lunâ candidissimâ,
Nobis indicata. *Bis.*

Regat Amicitia!
Curas expellamus, } *Bis.*
In amicis hilaris,
In opimis epulis,
Dulciter vivamus! *Bis.*

Sunt ubique socii,
Coronati palmâ; } *Bis.*
In Senatu consulent,
Illos musæ sustinent,
Fovet Mater Alma. *Bis.*

" Alpha Delta " gloriâ
Maximâ splendescat; } *Bis.*
Ad aeturnum floreat
Laureasque habeat;
Indies clarescat. *Bis.*

C. R. PALMER, Yale, 1855.

III.

VIVE, ALPHA DELTA PHI!

AIR—"*Lauriger Horatius.*"

Salve, Alpha Delta Phi,
Claritas aeterna,
Stellae est effluenti
Gloria superna.

> *Chorus*—Vive, Alpha Delta Phi,
> Vive, Alma Mater,
> Vive, stellaque coeli,
> Verus cordem frater.

In altaribus ignis
Vestales resplendent,
Et doctrinae animi
Tripodas defendent.

> *Chorus*—Vive, Alpha Delta Phi, etc.

Manus multae circum se
Frequenter contrahent,
Coronâ subnectere
Utinam gauderent.

> *Chorus*—Vive, Alpha Delta Phi, etc.

Vive, Alpha Delta Phi,
Cor unum amore,
Perdiu signa coeli,
Regant in splendore.

> *Chorus*—Vive, Alpha Delta Phi, etc.

D. N. VANDERVEER, Union, '63.

IV.

· MACTE ALPHA DELTA PHI.

AIR—"*Lauriger Horatius.*"

Macte Alpha Delta Phi,
  Gloriosis rebus,
Neque cedas tempori
  . Affluens diebus.

> *Chorus*—Vincula quam dulcia
>   Junctionis nostrae!
>   Jungant nos in sæcula,
>   Tuæ sorti sanctae.

Fulgeant argentea
  Cornua crescentis
Lunæ inter nubila,
  Nimbis violentis.

> *Chorus*—Vincula, etc.

Stella fida splendeat,
  Gloria cœlorum,
Surgens alte præbeat
  Multum gaudiorum.

> *Chorus*—Vincula, etc.

Igitur consortio,
  Vere quod amamus,
Comites magnifico
  Omnes gaudeamus.

> *Chorus*—·Vincula, etc.

J. H. REMINGTON, Brunonian, 1862.

V.

"QUÆ PRO NOBIS."

Nostra die opera
Quæ pro nobis levat?
Nocturna convivia,
Domina coronat?
Vincit illa nostra corda,
Nostros manus unâ;
Clara luce vivimus
Sub Falcatâ Lunâ.

Nostra Diva, pulchrior
Virgine Dianâ;
Corona est clarior,
Plura sua fana.
Clarior effulget Stella
Mane Lucifero;
Tristem Noctem luminat,
Bellior Hespero.

Mundus cœlus periant,
Vivat Alpha Delta!
Vulgus omnes mocreant,
Ridat Alpha Delta!
Sempiterna est et verna,
Vera sapientia,
Immortalis est amor,
Est Benevolentia!

FRANK SEWALL, Bowdoin.

VI.

HAIL TO THE STAR.

Air—"*Hail to the Chief.*"

Hail to the Star that is gleaming so brightly,
  Borne on our breasts as our ensign of pride,
Fairer to us than the thousands, that nightly
  Through the high heavens in majesty ride.
         May it be ever bright,
         May its effulgent light
     Ever gleam on us and gladden our way.
       Star of our hope and love,
       Long mayst thou shine above!
Hail to thee, fair one, bright star of our day!

Hail to the Crescent whose silvery glory
  Nightly grows broad on the zenith of fame;
Long be it honored in song and in story,
  Aye be its followers proud of their name!
        Manly the breasts that bear
        Our Crescent beaming fair;
    Warm are the hearts that are throbbing beneath.
       Ever our joyful song
       Ringeth forth clear and strong,
Hail to thee, Crescent! shine on us till death!

Crescent and Star! ye are emblems of brothers,
  Whose lives like the star, are resplendent and bright;
Of a fraternity which among others,
  Shines like the moon 'mid the jewels of night,
        Loved Alpha Delta Phi!
        Long may thy holy tie,
    Scholars and men in close sympathy bind.
       Bound in alliance strong,
       Ever we'll raise the song,
Hail to thee! union of heart and of mind!

               H. L. Boltwood, Amherst, 1853.

VII.

ALPHA DELTA, FOREVER.

AIR—"*Alabama Forever.*"

Let us swell the glad song, till its echoes around us
Fill the heart with its notes and with gladness surround
     us ;
Till these walls 'mid which pleasure so long has
     abounded,
Shall ring with the shout and the chorus resounded.
          Hurrah ! hurrah ! Alpha Delta, forever !
          Hurrah ! hurrah ! Alpha Delta, forever !

Our song is of triumph, victorious forever,
With no rival to fear, defeat we know never ;
Our aim always upward, our progress advancing,
Successes most perfect our glories enhancing.
          Hurrah ! hurrah ! etc.

As the past has been golden, immortal in story,
So the path of the future beams brilliant with glory ;
New honors are waiting, new beauties are o'er us,
And the noon of our brightness yet opens before us.
          Hurrah ! hurrah ! etc.

Thus, bold and unconquered, shall triumphs elate us,
And the bright course of glory undimmed shall await
     us ;
And brave Alpha Delta, bewitching as ever,
Shall reign 'mid her kindred a princess forever.
          Hurrah ! hurrah ! etc.

Alpha Delta ! Alpha Delta ! heaven's blessing attend
     her,
While we live, we will cherish, protect, and defend her ;
Our hearts swell with gladness whenever we name her,
And Queen of our thoughts we will ever proclaim her.
          Hurrah ! hurrah ! etc.

                              W. W. CRAPO, Yale, 1852.

VIII.

ROLL YE ON THE LOUD HUZZA.

AIR—"*Scots wha hae.*"

Roll ye on the loud huzza,
See arise yon orient Star
Born to spread the name afar
       Of Alpha Delta Phi!
Lo its radiant glories stand
Brightest of our native land,
Guiding on the mystic band
       Of the Alpha Delta Phi!

Suns may set to rise no more,
Night may stretch from shore to shore,
Ours is light, an endless store,
       In Alpha Delta Phi!
Hail! all hail! thou glorious dawn!
Welcome thrice auspicious morn;
Ignorance dies, and truth is born
       In Alpha Delta Phi!

Hear ye not the loud acclaim
Echoing forth from isle and main,
" Wisdom, love, and friendship reign
       In Alpha Delta Phi?"
Raise the pæan, shout the song;
Ring your anthem loud and long;
Bound in heart, we're brethren strong
       In Alpha Delta Phi!

ALEX. P. KETCHUM, Manhattan, 1858.

IX.

BENEATH OUR HALLOWED CRESCENT GLOW.

Air—" Those Evening Bells."

Beneath our hallowed crescent glow
   Warm hearts that drink life new and high,
From yon. fixed star, whose beams o'erflow
   The shrine of Alpha Delta Phi.

     Chorus—Of Delta Phi, of Delta Phi!
         We love the shrine of Delta Phi!

Here Science borrows Fancy's wing,
   And Romance looks through Reason's eye;
Here Genius learns to toil and sing
   The songs of cheerful industry.

     Chorus—Of Delta Phi, of Delta Phi,
         We love the songs of Delta Phi!

Here friendship, wit and genial mirth
   Banish with sunshine hours of gloom;
And when life meets its last of earth,
   Fond Memory decorates the tomb.

     Chorus—Old Delta Phi, old Delta Phi,
         We love the bonds of Delta Phi!

Then stand we, brothers, brave and strong,
   Lift we the star and crescent high,
Let Eloquence, and Love, and Song
   Give praise to Alpha Delta Phi.

     Chorus—To Delta Phi, to Delta Phi,
         Give praise to Alpha Delta Phi!

HAMILTON.

X.

THE STAR AND CRESCENT BRIGHT.

Air—"*O! for Wings to Soar;*" or, "*Prima Donna Song.*"

The Star and Crescent, bright,
  Forever in our sky,
Beam with a mild celestial light
  On Alpha Delta Phi.
The lingering forms of pleasures fled,
  May cause all other hearts to sigh;
But pure and noble joys are ours,
  In Alpha Delta Phi.

There is a chain which draws,
  Our hearts in friendship nigh;
It is the secret, golden bond
  Of Alpha Delta Phi.
Here Art and Genius both unite,
  To lift our aims and motives high;
A light to cheer the scholar's heart
  Is Alpha Delta Phi.

The laurel wreath of fame
  Upon her brow shall lie;
While victory shall crown the name
  Of Alpha Delta Phi.
In after years though we may part,
  We'll ne'er forget the sacred tie
That binds us closely heart to heart—
  'Tis Alpha Delta Phi.

Geo. S. Bishop, Amherst.

XI.

THE STUDENT'S GLEE.

AIR—"*Pirate's Glee.*"

Sing on! sing on! we love the chorus
  That's joined by hearts so strong and true;
The future, boys, is all before us,
  Its paths in glory we'll pursue.
Above our beating hearts is gleaming
  The star whose pure beam lights our way,
And still, o'er all our long path streaming,
  We see the Crescent's fadeless ray.

Sing on! sing on! we well may glory
  In Alpha Delta's old renown,
While countless tongues repeat her story,
  And countless hearts revere her crown.
She lives! our hearts are hers forever!
  She fades not with the fading years!
Her children will desert her never,
  Alike her own in smiles and tears.

Sing on! sing on! it still is morning
  In Alpha Delta's summer day,
All clouds of opposition scorning
  She brightens on her rising way.
And still while on in life we're moving,
  And day by day we leave this hour,
May Memory's record e'er be proving
  Old Alpha Delta's fadeless power.

W. O. STODDARD, Rochester Chapter, 1858.

XII.

WHEN THE EARNEST HEART.

A<small>IR</small>—"*My lodging is on the cold ground.*"

When the earnest heart turneth in sorrow away
    From the friends that allure to deceive,
And findeth no heart-love its own to repay,
    Alpha Delta its want will relieve.
For the trustful and strong here may fellowship find,
    Where refinement with manliness blends;
While around her dear altar our pledges we bind,
    That true hearts shall ne'er fail of true friends.

Here, too, may the scholar his young ardor bring,
    Whether genius or talent his share,
And in Science rise proudly on resolute wing,
    Or in Romance weave tapestries rare.
Whatever their gifts, whatever their skill,
    All they to whom honor is dear,
Alpha Delta will welcome, with hearty good will,
    To a brotherhood kind and sincere.

So with love and with songs Alpha Delta we crown,
    Alpha Delta, the genial and pure,
And the years as they roll shall add strength and re-
        nown,
    While Learning and Friendship endure.
Then brothers huzza! for the Crescent and Star,
    May their mild lustre never grow dim,
Till all noble spirits, both near and afar,
    Shall join in the glorious hymn.

S. S. G<small>ARDNER</small>, Bowdoin, 1855.

XIII.

COME ALL YE JOLLY STUDENTS.

Air—" *Benny Havens.*"

Come all ye jolly students, and join us in this song,
And loudly swell the chorus, its joyous notes prolong;
If any be who do not sing, they surely ought to try,
And see who'll give the loudest shout for Alpha Delta
    Phi.

Chorus.

If you seek for wit and humor, or need a helping hand,
You'll find them ready for you in an Alpha Delta band;
There's merriment and jollity, there's friendship true
    and high,
All fair and noble virtues meet in Alpha Delta Phi.

Chorus.

Drink to the shining Crescent and the Star of emerald
    green,
For long years they've been honored wherever they've
    been seen ;
For though the *profani* know not what they signify,
They know that he who wears them is an Alpha Delta
    Phi.

Chorus.

R. E. Taylor, Yale, 1854.

XIV.

SYMBOLS.

AIR—" *The rain upon the roof.*"

When the evening shadows gather
   Over Kenyon's silent halls
Bells are hushed and lights are twinkling
   Dreamily along the walls:—
Oh how sweet to steal in quiet
   Out beneath the winter sky,
Wend our way beyond the campus
   To thy temple Delta Phi.

From the swelling vault above us
   Every star that gems the night
Whispers: "In the field of action
   Let each son dispense thy light."
And our crescent's softened radiance
   Has a voice that will not die;
"Ever bright be ever modest,
   True to Alpha Delta Phi."

Treasuring up these sacred lessons
   Taught by nature to the heart,
In thy service we are chastened
   To perform a nobler part.
When around the shrine we circle,
   Every manly sparkling eye,
Tells by pure ambition strengthened,
   By thy symbols Delta Phi.

MURRAY DAVIS, Kenyon.

XV.

WHERE'ER THE FADELESS EMBLEMS.

Air—" *Dolly Day.*"

Where'er the fadeless Emblems of Alpha Delta shine
There gallant hearts and noble minds in friendship
firm entwine.
We are a band of brothers, united, tried, and true,
And happy the invited one who joins our chosen few.

    Chorus—O, glorious Alpha Delta Phi!
        We'll shout aloud thy praise;
       Thy sun the brightest in the sky,
        Shall shine through endless days.

Our banners ne'er shall waver before the strongest foe,
We'll always triumph over him, and ever mightier
grow;
We fear no frowning battlements, though towering
mountain high,
For victory's the Destiny of Alpha Delta Phi.

    Chorus—O, glorious Alpha Delta Phi!
        We'll shout aloud thy praise;
       Thy sun the brightest in the sky,
        Shall shine through endless days.

                         Brunonian.

XVI.

HAIL TO THEE.

AIR—"*Araby's Daughter.*"

Hail to thee, hail to thee, fair Alpha Delta,
   Our hearts' best affections are plighted to thee;
Never was Troubadour's lady-love fairer,
   Nymph of the forest or maid of the sea.

Chorus.

   Around thee we'll gather, while enemies threaten,
      Thy sons shall defend thee when danger is nigh;
   And far-distant shores shall re-echo the pæan,
      Long live Alma Mater and old Delta Phi!

Although the world knows not the tie that unites us,
   And sees but the casket inclosing the gem;
All honor the goddess whose tie so unites us,
   And envy the pleasures forbidden to them.

Chorus.

We'll cherish thee fondly till life's latest hour,
   And on our hearts' altar thine image enshrine;
Sweet memories of thee will by age gather power
   Like the sparkling nectar of Italy's vine.

Chorus.

C. R. PALMER, Yale, 1855.

XVII.

"JUVAT MEMINISSE."

Air—"A Wet Sheet and a Flowing Sea."

Fill up the beaker to the brim
  On this our festal night,
And clink each glass till its liquid rim
  Shall glow with sparkling light:
" Nunc gaudeamus "—let each care
  Be banished from this hour :
Old Time's gray locks once more shall wear
  The green sprig and the flower.

Chorus.
For we drink to the star whose beams shall shine
  As in the days gone by,
And we quaff the wine from the hearty vine
  Of Alpha Delta Phi.

Not Old Falernian can compare,
  Nor juice of San Peray,
With the blood of our grape so rich and rare,
  And its odorous bouquet;
It has the true smack of the heart,
  The flavor of the soul,
And it fires the veins with a subtler art
  Than the spell of the Lesbian bowl.

Chorus.
Then drink to the star whose beams still shine
  As in the days gone by,
We quaff the wine from the glorious vine
  Of Alpha Delta Phi.

There is no head-ache in this wine,
  No heart-ache in its lees,
But beams divine through the liquor shine,
  And heaven-born charities ;
    2*

The graces of the mind which lend
   To life its charm and zest,
And golden dreams and memories blend
   In the draught forever blest.

Chorus.
Then drink to the star whose beams still shine
   As in the days gone by,
We quaff the wine from the fragrant vine
   Of Alpha Delta Phi.

" Cras iterabimus æquor,"
   Yet we will not forget
That friendship which shall know no flaw,
   That star which ne'er shall set;
The winds may pipe and clouds may pass
   Across Life's fitful sea,
We'll crush the grape and clink the glass
   To the hours of memory.

Chorus.
Then drink to the star whose beams still shine
   As in the days gone by,
We quaff the wine from the stout old vine
   Of Alpha Delta Phi.

And when at last our hearts grow chill
   And turn to silent dust,
We shall not die, for brave hearts still
   Shall keep the ancient trust;
The vine shall wear its blooms of Spring,
   The star its radiance cast,
And still to Memory's cup shall cling
   The bees-wing of the past.

Chorus.
Then drink to the star whose beams still shine
   As in the days gone by,
There is no wine like the juice of the vine
   Of Alpha Delta Phi.

HENRY CLAY WHITAKER.

XVIII.

COME, BROTHERS, AND JOIN US.

Air—"*Alabama Again.*"

Come, brothers, and join us to swell the glad chorus,
  Let each fill the air with a glorious strain;
With hearts all united and banners victorious,
  We'll shout Alpha Delta, Alpha Delta again.

Chorus.
Alpha Delta again, Alpha Delta again;
With hearts all united, and banners victorious
We'll shout Alpha Delta, Alpha Delta again.

The Star and the Crescent, all glowing with beauty,
  Shine out with a radiance none others attain,
And silently, earnestly, urge us in duty,
  To shout Alpha Delta, Alpha Delta again.

Chorus—Alpha Delta again, etc.

Full many a gem we have laid on her altar—
  Full many a vow we have made at her shrine;
And chaplets of beauty we've wreathed to exalt her,
  To crown Alpha Delta, our goddess divine!

Chorus—Alpha Delta again, etc.

If envy assail her with breath of detraction,
  Or evil-eyed malice with venomous darts,
We'll bravely defend her in life's every action,
  Beloved Alpha Delta, the queen of our hearts.

Chorus—Alpha Delta again, etc.

Then brothers anew let us swell the glad chorus,
  Let heart answer heart in the joyous refrain;
While Crescent and Star light the pathway before us,
  All hail Alpha Delta, Alpha Delta again.

Chorus—Alpha Delta again, etc.

H. J., Hamilton.

XIX.

STARLIGHT CHORUS.

Arranged from Rossini.

Alpha Delta, we adore thee,
　Thou hast won our hearts' best love;
And with praises round thee meeting
Praises long and loud repeating,
　Sing we to the stars above.

Hark! the stars responsive answer,
　With a shout to cheer us on;
From each golden throat now welling
Into choral grandeur swelling,
　" Courage till the crown be won!"

Alpha Delts! arise! be earnest!
　Strive with all our greatest powers;
Soon we yield our place to others,
Work, then, while we may, O, brothers,
　Soon the victory shall be ours!

H. KINGSBURY, Yale, 1863.

XX.

STAR AND CRESCENT.

Air—"*Allan Waters.*"

O, do you see in yon blue arch,
    The bright and glorious star of even
Lead out the hosts that nightly march
    Across the boundless plain of heaven?

Behold a symbol of our aim,
    Set high above the aim of others,—
The fairest name, the purest fame,
    That wreaths a human brow, my brothers.

And see you too yon crescent light,
    As modest as a wooed maiden,
That comes up each successive night
    With richer freight of glory laden?

O, that's a symbol of the way
    Our lives must differ from all others,—
The present may do for to-day,
    The morn must find us more, my brothers.

The star rides up its shining arc,
    And brighter burns until descended;
The moon, at first a silver mark,
    Comes out at last a planet splendid.

O, these are pointers to the path
    Which leads to higher heights than others,
In all the strife of human life,
    A silent, constant, growth, my brothers.

                                    Peninsular.

XXI.

BRIGHT SHINING O'ER US.

AIR—"*John Brown.*"

Bright shining o'er us are the crescent and the star,
Our pathway before us they illumine from afar ;
Join, then, the chosen brethren, wheresoe'er you are,
  For Alpha Delta Phi.

Chorus.
Glory, glory to our union,
Glory, glory to our union,
Of hearts and hands the sweet communion
  In Alpha Delta Phi.

Glad is the meeting, and each brother's heart to-night
Quickly is beating 'neath the star and crescent bright;
The solemn vows repeating that shall bind us to the
  right,
  In Alpha Delta Phi.

Chorus.
Glory, glory to the union,
Glory, glory to the union,
Of hearts and hands the sweet communion
  In Alpha Delta Phi.

May the star shine forever and the crescent never wane,
Our ties never sever, but in constancy remain,
And we'll shout altogether as we raise the glad refrain
  Of Alpha Delta Phi.

Chorus.
Glory, glory to the union,
Glory, glory to the union,
Of hearts and hands the sweet communion
  In Alpha Delta Phi.

CHAS. E. SPRAGUE, Union.

XXII.

COME, COME, TRUE ALPHA DELTA.

AIR—"*Am I not fondly thine own.*"

Come, come true Alpha Deltas,
  Join, join in a festival song,
Hearts, hearts unite in the chorus
  That ringeth out hearty and strong.
    Chorus—Shout, shout, shout, shout,
        Shout for our loved Alpha Delta,
      Shout, shout, shout, shout,
        Shout for our dear Delta Phi.

Some, some whose voices have echoed,
  Here, here in days that are gone,
Now, now rest from their labors—
  Brothers, their duties are done.
    Chorus—Gone, gone, gone, gone,
        Gone from our loved Alpha Delta,
      Gone, gone, gone, gone,
        Gone from our dear Delta Phi.

Hearts, hearts loving and loyal,
  Meet, meet round her to-night,
Thoughts, thoughts of those who have left us,
  But render our pleasures more bright.
    Chorus—Here, here, here, here,
        Here round our loved Alpha Delta,
      Here, here, here, here,
        Here round our dear Delta Phi.

And when, silent, unthrobbing,
  Our hearts rest 'neath the sod,
Feet, feet as loving and loyal
  Shall tread in the paths we have trod.
    Chorus—Shout, shout, shout, shout,
        Shout for our loved Alpha Delta,
      Shout, shout, shout, shout,
        Shout for our dear Delta Phi.

XXIII.

MARTIAL CHORUS.

(Donizetti.)

I.

Fair is our golden crescent and bright,
    Fair is our star that glitters on high;
Witching and soft falls answering light,
    Fair eyes grow sparkling for old Delta Phi.

II.

Around her strong hearts beat fearless and free ;
    Subjects of hers her rivals shall prove,
Glorious and bright her pathway shall be,
    Proud Alpha Delta, the home of our love.

III.

Long in her smile shall eloquence glow,
    Burning with flame undying; and long
Through her old halls right gayly shall flow
    Music, and mirth, and festival song.

IV.

For true hearts beat ever proudly for thee ;
    Queen of the sky thy crescent shall prove ;
Glory and light around thee shall be,
    Fair Alpha Delta, the home of our love.

                J. B. MITCHELL, Yale, 1863.

XXIV.

FAITHFUL AND TRUE.

AIR—"*Sparkling and Bright.*"

Faithful and true to our chosen few,
 At the merry hour of meeting,
We gather all in our beauteous hall,
 To exchange a brother's greeting.

Chorus.

And ere adieu, our vows renew,
 To friends as fixed to meet us,
As the stars that glow in the heaven's bow,
 And at evening kindly greet us.

And who can rue, what here we do
 In holy love, and plighted
In friendship sure, with purpose pure,
 By Star and Crescent lighted.
 Chorus—Then ere adieu, etc.

Our ties are new, but life is due
 To aught that can divide them ;
And memory's power shall guard the hour,
 When earth's embrace shall hide them.
 Chorus—Then ere adieu, etc.

BOWDOIN.

3

XXV.

COME, BROTHERS, LET US BANISH.

Air—"*Nelly Gray.*"

Come, Brothers, let us banish every gloomy thought
  to-night—
  Let us now bid adieu to every sigh ;
Let each voice join the chorus, and let every heart be
  light
  While we sing of old Alpha Delta Phi.

Chorus.

O Alpha Delta Phi ! brave old Alpha Delta Phi !
  We'll sing of thy glories ever more ;
While the Star and the Crescent shed their glories
    through the sky
  And the waves of old ocean beat the shore.

With joy we have gathered here, a true and faithful
  band,
  Round the shrine of our Alpha Delta Phi ;
And our hearts are knit closer as we clasp each friendly
  hand,
  And pledge truth and friendship till we die.

Chorus.

When the weary week is ended, and its labors all are
  o'er—
  When its cares and its troubles are laid by—
How we'll love then to gather in our cheerful hall once
  more,
  And sing of old Alpha Delta Phi.

Chorus.

B. M. CUTCHEON, Peninsular.

XXVI.

HURRA FOR ALPHA DELTA.

AIR—"*Hurrah for old New England.*"

Let strains of joyous music fill
Our souls with pleasure high ;
As, hand in hand, our faith we pledge
To grand old Delta Phi.

Aye, firm in purpose, true in soul,
At genial friendship's call ;
Together, 'neath the crescent's light,
We'll either stand or fall.

Chorus.   Hurrah for Alpha Delta,   } *bis.*
And her noble band of sons.

The hour brings joy and rousing cheer
To souls with toil oppressed ;
Like coolness, wafted on the breeze
From summer ocean's breast.

Then bury every hostile thought,
The altar fire draw nigh,
And warm anew each soul with love
Of dear old Delta Phi !
Chorus.

C. O. T.

XXVII.

COME, BROTHERS, JOIN THE CHORUS.

Air—"*Benny Havens.*"

Come, Brothers, join the chorus, loud let your voices
  sound,
To praise this glorious circle where love and joy
  abound ;
We'll raise the shout of gladness, we'll fill our goblets
  high,
And the toast shall be, " The friends we love, and
  Alpha Delta Phi !"
                And Alpha Delta Phi, etc.

Now the busy day is ended, we have banished every
  care,
The college halls are vacant, and each grave professor's
  chair ;
Latin, Greek, and Mathematics we have willingly laid
  by,
And merrily we'll rally round our Alpha Delta Phi—
                Our Alpha Delta Phi, etc.

There are homes whose pleasant memories we cherish
  day by day,
There are loved ones pure and beautiful, and kindred
  far away ;
But here's the *student's* hearthstone whose fires shall
  never die,
For we'll keep them brightly burning in Alpha Delta
  Phi—
                In Alpha Delta Phi, etc.

XXVIII.

THE SUN HAS GONE DOWN.

Air—"*Juvallera.*"

The sun has gone down and the daylight is past,
The dark shades of evening are gathering fast,
Come brothers, the hour and the day us invite,
To the pleasures of old Alpha Delta to-night.
   Chorus—Juvallera, Juvallera,
     Ju—valle—valle—valle—ra. *Bis.*

When, weary and worn with the cares of the week,
An hour's release from our toils we would seek,
With the joy of the sailor whose haven is nigh,
To old Alpha Delta we merrily hie.
   Chorus—Juvallera, etc.

Oh ! where are the scornful who tell us of life,
" 'Tis a sea that is rayless, with sorrowing rife ;"
For the Star and the Crescent rise bright o'er the wave,
In darkness to guide, and in peril to save.
   Chorus—Juvallera, etc.

Our life's full of joy that's as lasting and pure
As the snows that on Himmalya's summits endure,
For from old Alpha Delta there ceaselessly flow
All the pleasures that man can inherit below.
   Chorus—Juvallera, etc.

When years have flown by, and in manhood's full
  might,
We are called, one and all, our life's battle to fight,
When sorrows oppress, and when laurels we earn,
To old Alpha Delta fond memory shall turn.
   Chorus—Juvallera, etc.

           Yale, 1855.

3*

XXIX.

COME TO THE SPOT.

AIR—"*The Old Gum Tree.*"

Come to the spot so dear,
  Where the tried and the true are found ;
Come join in the festive cheer,
  And loud your voices sound.
    Solo—Bright beam the lights around us,
      The walls in beauty smile ;
    Gay mirth and joy surround us,
      And chain our souls the while.
  Chorus—Then come to the spot so dear, etc.

The place we love it well,
  Its charms to us are sweet ;
For mirth and pleasure dwell
  Within this safe retreat.
    Solo—Without the wind may whistle,
      The tempest mutter loud ;
    For these we care but little,
      When with this jolly crowd.
  Chorus—Then come to the spot so dear, etc.

Bright beams the sparkling eye,
  Our hearts with gladness bound,
And the moments quickly fly,
  As the jovial song goes round.
    Solo—Here in life's rosy morning,
      Ere time's dull cares are felt,
    Our hearts all sorrow scorning,
      Shall feast in Alpha Delt.
  Chorus—Then come to the spot so dear.

W. W. CRAPO, Yale, 1852.

XXX.

LOVED ALPHA DELTA PHI.

AIR—" *Vive l'America.*"

Fair Alpha Delta, honored afar,
Bright o'er thy crescent gloweth thy star;
Pure and unfading, gemming the night,
Cheering each heart with their radiant light.
For them we'll live, beneath them we'll die,
Proudly their praises we'll ring to the sky,
Throughout the world our watchword shall be,
Loved Alpha Delta Phi, blessings on thee!

Where'er thy sons shall rest or shall roam,
Still shall the crescent remind them of home;
Still shall the star with undying ray,
Gather sweet memories over their way.
For thee we'll live, beside thee we'll die,
Proudly we'll shout thy dear name to the sky,
Throughout the world our watchword shall be,
Loved Alpha Delta Phi, blessings on thee!

Brave Alpha Delta, glorious and free,
All the world o'er we're loyal to thee;
Queen of our hearts whom none can dethrone,
Ever the sway of thy beauty we own.
Braving for thee all danger and scorn,
Onward forever thy name shall be borne,
Throughout the world our watchword shall be,
Loved Alpha Delta Phi, blessings on thee.

HAMILTON.

XXXI.

WITH HEARTS AND HANDS UNITED.

Air—"*Dixie's Land.*"

Away from the eye and ear of others,
Here we are, a band of brothers,
  Then hurrah, hip hurrah, hip hurrah, Delta Phi.
Of the mystic ties that ever bind us,
Star and crescent well remind us,
  Then hurrah, hip hurrah, hip hurrah, Delta Phi.
 Chorus—With hearts and hands united, away, away,
    We'll raise the song our notes prolong
     To shout for Alpha Delta;
     Hurrah, hurrah, hurrah, for Alpha Delta,
     Hurrah, hurrah, hurrah, for Alpha Delta.

When care and trouble worry and grieve us,
Nolens volens, here they leave us,
  Then hurrah, hip hurrah, hip hurrah, Delta Phi;
So brothers, all, let us here together,
Wish her youth and luck forever,
  Then hurrah, hip hurrah, hip hurrah, Delta Phi.
 Chorus—With hearts and hands united, etc.

Thirty-two was the year that she was born in,
Ushering in a glorious morning,
  Then hurrah, hip hurrah, Delta Phi;
And, as her sons, we'll shout the chorus,
Till the heavens echo o'er us,
  Then hurrah, hip hurrah, hip hurrah, Delta Phi.
 Chorus—With hearts and hands united, etc.

All hail to the star and glowing crescent,
Alpha Delta, Heaven bless it;
  Then hurrah, hip hurrah, hip hurrah, Delta Phi.
May Friendship, Fame and Fortune attend her,
Every arm and heart defend her,
  Then hurrah, hip hurrah, hip hurrah, Delta Phi.
 Chorus—With hearts and hands united, etc.

         HAMILTON.

XXXII.

A GAY, GALLANT SHIP.

Air—" *One Friday morning we set sail.*"

A gay, gallant ship, with a well-tried crew,
　Is the Alpha Delta Phi,
With form so fair and timbers true,
　And a flag that floats on high, on high,
　And a flag that floats on high.

, *Chorus.*

Then call all hands, and spread all sail,
　The roaring gale defy,
The moon and star will ne'er grow pale
　O'er the flag of the Alpha Delta Phi, Delta Phi,
　O'er the flag of the Alpha Delta Phi.

We fear not the gale, we fear not the foe,
　The storm-king's might we'll try,
With flashing guns we'll scare from the seas
　The foes of the Alpha Delta Phi, Delta Phi,
　The foes of the Alpha Delta Phi.

Chorus.

Then call all hands, and spread all sail,
　The roaring gale defy,
The moon and star will ne'er grow pale
　O'er the flag of the Alpha Delta Phi, Delta Phi,
　O'er the flag of the Alpha Delta Phi.

A. B. JUDSON, Brunonian.

XXXIII.

THE STAR OF ALPHA DELTA.

AIR—"*Benny Havens.*"

The Star of Alpha Delta, the brightest star of night,
And ever-waxing Crescent with pure, unfading light,
Now shine in beauty o'er us as we raise our voices high,
To sing the welcome chorus of our Alpha Delta Phi.
Our Alpha Delta Phi, etc.

With cordial hands extended, we welcome to our home
These true and loving brothers who through the vale
have come,
And sing the joys that thrill us all within the social tie
Where mind and heart the pillars are of Alpha Delta
Phi.
Of Alpha Delta Phi, etc.

In friendship true and holy our hearts united are ;
And Alpha Delta's glory, the Crescent and the Star,
Shall urge us on to duty while they help us each to vie
To add new strength and beauty to our Alpha Delta Phi.
To our Alpha Delta Phi, etc.

XXXIV.

OUR BADGE.

Air—"*Auld Lang Syne.*".

'Tis well to sing a song to-night,
  And ask the question why
The *badge* is thus, those brethren wear
  Called Alpha Delta Phi.

So pure their work, their high designs,
  The lights of yonder sky
Have deigned to give symbolic signs
  To Alpha Delta Phi.

The *waxing moon, the flaming star*,
  While passing others by,
Held back their swift ethereal car
  For Alpha Delta Phi.

And thus the brightness of their rays
  Descending from on high,
Impressed the *image* of their gaze
  On Alpha Delta Phi.

And hence the *truth* these signs impart,
  The *worth* they signify,
Beam from the *badge*, and warm the heart
  Of Alpha Delta Phi.

N. W. WILDER.

XXXV.

OUR ALPHA DELTA PHI.

AIR—"*Annie Lisle.*"

Would you know the lights that fairest
    Deck the azure sky?
They're the Star and silvery Crescent
    Of our Delta Phi.
Window lights in heaven's bright mansions
    Gleaming through the night,
Their soft rays o'er Alpha Delta
    Shed a golden light.
Chorus—Beam o'er us, Star and Crescent,
        Guide us till we die,
        Each a brother loving truly
        Alpha Delta Phi.

Would you kneel around an altar
    Whence ascends on high
Friendship's incense?—it is burning
    In our Delta Phi.
Ever bright the fires are glowing,
    And the sweet perfume
Of that holy friendship lingers
    Round each brother's tomb.
    Chorus—Beam o'er us, etc.

Would you join a band of brothers,
    Where each beaming eye
Tells of pleasures never ceasing,
    Join our Delta Phi.
Hand to hand we stand united,
    And from heart to heart
Runs a bond of plighted friendship
    Time can never part.
    Chorus—Beam o'er us, etc.

H. L. CHAPMAN, Bowdoin.

XXXVI.

AS THE WELCOME NIGHT RECALLS DELIGHT.

Air—"*Sparkling and Bright.*"

As the welcome night recalls delight,
   And the joyful hour of meeting,
With hearty cheer do we gather here
   To exchange a merry greeting.
         Chorus.
Then sing to-night, let hearts be light,
   The world is bright before us;
And our souls are brave, for then shall wave
   The Star and Crescent o'er us.

Oh! if we e'er might tarry here,
   What joy in life should meet us,
Where hands should clasp in friendly grasp,
   And kindly welcomes greet us.
   Chorus—Then sing to-night, etc.

Let's banish strife, the broils of life,
   Leave jealousies to others,
Joined heart and hand together stand
   A band of faithful brothers.
   Chorus—Then sing to-night, etc.

                       H. M. U., Peninsular.

4

XXXVII.

THE STAR OF ALPHA DELTA.

Air — " *Open the Cupboard.*"

There is a star in our sky, brothers,
Towards which we turn our eye, brothers,
And govern our actions by, brothers,
  'Tis the star of Alpha Delta.

That star is forever near, brothers,
Though around us all is drear, brothers,
It gives us nothing to fear, brothers,
  The star of Alpha Delta.

Success to her let us sing, brothers,
And loud let the chorus ring, brothers,
To her we will ever cling, brothers,
  Our star of Alpha Delta.

Then the star and crescent bright, brothers,
We will always keep in sight, brothers,
They will guide us in the right, brothers,
  Long live our Alpha Delta.

      A. O. Treat, Williams, '63.

XXXVIII.

ALPHA DELTAS, RAISE THE SONG.

Air—'' 'Landlord, fill the flowing bowl.''

Alpha Deltas, raise the song—
  Banish care and sorrow ;
Long and loud the strain prolong,
  Until the dawning morrow !
    Chorus — Alpha Delta Phi, my boys,
          The theme of song and story—
          While the Star and Crescent shine,
          We'll ever sing her glory.

Once again we here renew
  The bonds that none may sever ;
Tried and true—a chosen few—
  Alpha Delts forever !
    Chorus — Alpha Delta Phi, etc.

Bright afar now shines the Star,
  And rides the Crescent o'er us ;
Roll along the loud huzza,
  And raise the swelling chorus !
    Chorus — Alpha Delta Phi, etc.

M. MARBLE, Rochester, 1855.

XXXIX.

OUR ALPHA DELTA HOME.

Air — "*Sweet Home.*"

O'er the wide face of earth, though the Alpha Delta
    roam,
No place can he find like his Alpha Delta Home,
A charm from the past seems to hallow us there,
A heart and a hope that ne'er nerve us elsewhere.

Chorus.

Home! home! dear college home!
There is no place on earth like our Alpha Delta home.

And, week after week, as we joyously meet,
And each true Alpha Delta our coming shall greet,
We will spend the best hours of each long College year
With the warm hearts and brave hearts that welcome
    us here.

Chorus.

Home! home! dear college home!
There is no place on earth like our Alpha Delta home.

The homes of our youth bring their memories there—
Its love-hallowed hearth their affection shall share;
The tempter shall call us to leave it, in vain!
O! give me the hands of my brethren again.

Chorus.

Home! home! dear college home!
There is no place on earth like our Alpha Delta home.

W. O. STODDARD.

XL.
SHOUT FOR ALPHA DELTA.

AIR—" *The Daughter of the Cure.*"

Come, brothers all, and join our song,
  And shout for Alpha Delta ;
The name shall echo loud and long,
  Hurrah for Alpha Delta!
Her sons, though few, are tried and true,
  Our bond is like a brother's ;
Our love from her will never turn,
  Her ties are like no others.

Chorus.

Come, brothers all, and join our song,
  And shout for Alpha Delta ;
The name shall echo loud and long,
  Hurrah for Alpha Delta!

The Star so bright, the Crescent white,
  The signs of Alpha Delta,
We'll never, never, lose from sight;
  We'll think of Alpha Delta.
So, brothers, let your shout be loud,
  And join ye now the chorus,
Of her we surely may be proud,
  All others fade before us.

Chorus.

And when we all have left these shades,
  Have left our Alma Mater,
There's one remembrance never fades,
  Of thee ! fair Alpha Delta.
Throughout our lives we'll think of thee,
  We'll glory in thy glory,
And tell to ages yet to be,
  Thine honor and thy story.

Chorus.

Dedicated to MANHATTAN, by N. L.

4*

XLI.

FAIR ALPHA DELTA.

AIR—"*Ever be Happy.*"

Fair Alpha Delta, in glory enshrined,
  Hail to thy emerald Star!
Long may its beams, with our Crescent combined,
  Illumine our path from afar.

Chorus.

Ne'er let dishonor thy fair fame destroy,
Nor malice, nor envy, our pleasure alloy;
Fair Alpha Delta, our hearts' pride and joy,
  Hail to thy glorious Star!
  Hail, hail to thy glorious Star! *Bis.*

Amid college duties, the world's busy strife,
  Our allegiance we'll still own to thee;
And if e'er we prove false to our trust during life,
  Despised by thy sons may we be.

Chorus.

Fair Alpha Delta, let those scoff who know
  Nought of thy virtues or worth;
And may thy loved symbols bright glory bestow
  On the noblest and best of this earth.

Chorus.

W. H. L., Manhattan. '65.

XLII.

Der Stern des Abendlandes.

Seht nach dem fernen Abendland,
Wo viele Sterne scheinen,
Vorzüglich unter ihrem Rang
Erblickt man doch den einen,
    Den nennt man Alpha Delta,
    Erhabne Alpha Delta
    Ha ha ha ha ha (bis)
    Die Alpha Delta Phi.

Wie hochbeglückt diejenigen
Im Streit und Weltgetümmel,
Gekrönt von ihrem klaren Schein
Herab vom heitren Himmel,
    Die Söhne Alpha Deltas,—u. f. w.

Wir leben in der fel'gen Huld
Des Halbmonds filbernen Strahlen,
Vereinigt je wenn auch getrennt,
Ein Herz, das Herz von allen
    Die Söhne Alpha Deltas,—2c.

Laß kommen Widerwärtigkeit,
Feindseligkeit und Müh'
Doch Brüder sind wir allezeit
Fest schauend in die Höh'
    Wo wohnet Alpha Delta,—2c.

Ihr' mystische geheime Kraft
Die uns verbindet hier,
Sei Stärke uns und Lebensgeist
Zu siegen für und für.
    Dann jauchzet Alpha Delta!
    Heil! Heil Dir! Alpha Delta!
    Ha ha ha ha ha (bis)
    Heil Alpha Delta Phi!

             J. H. Brooking.

XLIII.

COME, BROTHERS, DRIVE DULL CARE AWAY.

AIR — "*Few Days.*"

Come, brothers, send dull care away,
  Hurrah! hurrah!
And merrily sing till dawn of day,
  In old Delta Phi.
    Chorus — Shout for Alpha Delta,
        Hurrah! hurrah!
      Shout for Alpha Delta,
        Hip, hip, hurrah!
      Out let the chorus ring,
        Hurrah! hurrah!
      Join all the praise to sing,
        Of old Delta Phi.

How many pleasant memories—
  Hurrah! hurrah!
In after years will frequent rise,
  Of old Delta Phi!

How, when there comes a   night—
  Hurrah! hurrah!
We'll call to mind our old delight,
  In old Delta Phi!

And oft we'll tell our pretty wives,
  Hurrah! hurrah!
How we enjoyed our college lives
  And old Delta Phi!

Then, brothers, sing right merrily,
  Hurrah! hurrah!
O! what a jolly crowd are we,
  In old Delta Phi!

YALE, 1855.

XLIV.

THE STAR AND CRESCENT,

AIR — " *Sheepskin.* "

Come, brothers, let us watch the sky,
  At the horizon gaze,
And see the emerald Star rise high,
  In full resplendent blaze.
Ah! there she is—a beacon light,
  To guide us on our way,
With Alpha Delta rays as bright
  As sunbeams at mid-day.

Look now upon yon crescent moon,
  So silvery and so fair ;
Say, think ye that the " Lord of Noon "
  Hath beauties half as rare ?
Some spots there are upon her face,
  But know ye what they mean ?
'Tis Alpha Delta Phi you trace
  Amidst the glorious sheen.

Oh! may our Star forever shine!
  Our Crescent never wane!
And may they ever light the shrine
  Of our loved goddess queen!
May cords of love and truth unite
  To form our " mystic tie!"
And may they bind us to the right
  And Alpha Delta Phi!

M. J. BLAKELEY, Manhattan, 1858.

XLV.

THE MYSTIC CRYSTAL.

Air — "*Benny Havens.*"

When Zeus his ivory scepter took,
   And built his throne on high,
From jeweled crown he dropped the "star"
   Of Alpha Delta Phi.
In settings pure and true and strong,
   We clasped it with our love,
And kept the mystic crystal
   He sent us from above.

Here streams abroad the talisman,
   God's smile is in its glow ;
Its lustre shedding fresh and pure,
   And bright as sunlit snow.
We'll tell its wondrous meaning,
   Its praises we will sing,
And bless the sacred day that brought
   The god's first offering.

Here, Learning spreads her spangled zone,
   Here Delphic honors meet,
And round the chancel of our faith
   The Graces stand complete.
While reigning o'er the sacred dome
   That spans our social sky,
The Star the brightest shines abroad,
   O'er Alpha Delta Phi.

On altars of true virtue,
   We'll offer up the gem,
And place the star we love so well
   In Beauty's diadem ;
We'll wreath it with devotion,
   Its charms shall never die ;
The Star, the bright and beautiful,
   Of Alpha Delta Phi.

D. N. Vanderveer, Union, 1863.

XLVI.

WE'RE A GALLANT BAND OF BROTHERS.

AIR—" There's a Yellow Rose of Texas."

We're a gallant band of brothers, as ever wove the tie
That binds for aye the youthful heart in Alpha Delta Phi.
Fair Learning is our Priestess—her altars we'll uphold;
For love unites each hero breast around her spangled fold.

Chorus.

Oh! Alpha Delt, with Star so bright, and Crescent flashing high,
We'll bow beneath thy holy fane and worship till we die.
We'll tell of all our high-born hopes—we'll sing our songs of glee,
And pledge to all thy loyal sons a home in Tennessee.

Here proudly rears, in laurel'd fame, our temple of the sky;
Here flames abroad the vestal fire of Alpha Delta Phi,
And high that star-born music from out her pillar'd aisle,
For ever breathes our plighted faith which naught shall e'er defile.

*Chorus—*Oh! Alpha Delt, with Star so bright, etc.

Fore'er yon jewel'd altars, where evening shadows lie,
Shall emblemize the hidden joys of Alpha Delta Phi;
Their light shall gild our college years, nor with their joys depart,
But weave each blessed thought around this Mecca of the heart.

*Chorus—*Oh! Alpha Delt, with Star so bright, etc.

And e'er yon rosy fingers, amid the twilight sky,
Shall write the name, in blushing light, of Alpha Delta Phi.
Then fling aloft her banner wild, we'll wreathe it with our love.
A sentinel to guard it, all rustling proud above.

*Chorus—*Oh! Alpha Delt, with Star so bright, etc.

And though the nation quivers in waves of faction high,
We'll man our UNION vessel of Alpha Delta Phi.
We'll rally closer to her mast, and, with heroic lip,
Exclaim, with gallant Lawrence—"Oh, don't give up the ship!"

*Chorus—*Oh! Alpha Delt, with Star so bright, etc.

ALEXANDER ALLISON, Cumberland, 1861.

XLVII.

HERE'S TO ALPHA DELTA.

AIR—" *Drink it Down.*"

Here's to Alpha Delta, } *Bis.*
   Drink it down!
Here's to Alpha Delta,
In triumphant strains exalt her !
   Drink it down. *Bis.*
   Drink it down—down—down !

Here's to Alma Mater, } *Bis.*
   Drink it down!
Here's to Alma Mater,
And to each true-hearted Frater !
   Drink it down. *Bis.*
   Drink it down—down—down !

Here's to the emerald Star, } *Bis.*
   Drink it down!
Here's to the emerald Star,
Shedding radiance near and far !
   Drink it down. *Bis.*
   Drink it down—down—down !

Here's to the shining Crescent, } *Bis.*
   Drink it down!
Here's to the shining Crescent,
In our sky it's ever present!
   Drink it down. *Bis.*
   Drink it down—down—down !

Once more to Alpha Delta, } *Bis.*
   Drink it down !
Once more to Alpha Delta,
And in louder strains exalt her !
   Drink it down. *Bis.*
   Drink it down—down—down !

M. MARBLE, Rochester, 1855.

XLVIII.

VIVE LA COMPAGNIE.

Air—" *Vive la Compagnie.*"

Come all ye good Alpha Delts, tune up your throats,
            Vive la compagnie ;
And lustily sing to the jolly old notes,
            Vive la compagnie.
        Vive la vive la vive la va,
        Vive la vive la vive la va,
        Vive la va, hop sa sa,
            Vive la compagnie.

Away with the musty old books of the sages,
            Vive la compagnie ;
For warm hearts and loving need no printed pages,
            Vive la compagnie.
            Chorus.

So a health to each other let's drink one and all,
            Vive la compagnie ;
In friendship together whate'er may befall
            Vive la compagnie.
            Chorus.

And a health to our symbols, the Crescent and Star,
            Vive la compagnie ;
And a health to their bearers wherever they are,
            Vive la compagnie.
            Chorus.

And last to herself, our old Delta Phi,
            Vive la compagnie ;
With a jovial shout and a goblet filled high,
            Vive la compagnie.
            Chorus.

                        F. S., Bowdoin, 1858.

5

XLIX.

IN GOLDEN MYSTIC CIRCLE.

AIR—" *Robin Adair.*"

In golden mystic circle,
    Alpha Delta, Alpha Delta;
And with its holiest bands,
    Alpha Delta, Alpha Delta;
Firmly the cords of love
Unite our hearts and hands,
    Alpha, Alpha Delta Phi.

With honor's glist'ning myrtle,
    Alpha Delta, Alpha Delta,
She wreaths each fair young brow,
    Alpha Delta, Alpha Delta ;
Our Star and shining Crescent
Wax ever brighter now,
    Alpha, Alpha Delta Phi.

Some on the battle-field,
    Alpha Delta, Alpha Delta;
Some in the senate's hall,
    Alpha Delta, Alpha Delta;
Where'er Freedom summons,
There ready come we all,
    Alpha, Alpha Delta Phi.

Then come! onward! upward!
    Alpha Delta, Alpha Delta;
To where our gleaming Star,
    Alpha Delta, Alpha Delta;
Burns with waxing Crescent
Heavenward! come, you, afar !
    Alpha, Alpha Delta Phi.

C. GARDNER, Williams, 1864.

L.

ANOTHER BUSY WEEK HAS PAST.

AIR—" *Litoria.*"

Another busy week has past,
    Swee de la we dum bum,
And   night has come at last,
    Swee de la wee dum bum ;
Then brothers lay your studies by,
    Swee de la wee tchu hi ra sa,
And shout for Alpha Delta Phi,
    Swee de la wee dum bum.
  Litoria, Litoria, swee de la wee tchu hi ra sa.
  Litoria, Litoria, swee de la wee dum bum.

The evening Star sheds beams of peace,
    Sweet de la wee dum bum,
The Crescent's silver horns increase ;
    Swee de la wee dum bum.
And would you know the reason why ?
    Swee de la wee tchu hi ra sa,
They're signs of Alpha Delta Phi,
    Swee de la wee dum bum.
  Litoria, etc.

What wealth is there in any land,
    Swee de la wee dum bum,
What gems upon the ocean sand,
    Swee de la wee dum bum,
That could with all their beauty buy,
    Swee de la wee tchu hi ra sa,
Our hearts from Alpha Delta Phi ?
    Swee de la wee dum bum.
  Litoria, etc.

HENRY F. COLBY, Brunonian, '62.

LI.

WORK'S OVER AND DONE.

Air—" *Carry Me 'Long.*"

Work's over and done,
  Then off to our halls, away ;
Where story and song the hours prolong,
  Till the night gives place to the day.
    Heigh, boys ! raise the strain,
      And let it echo free ;
    The songs we love the praises of
      Our Alpha Delta Phi.

Greek's well in its place,
  Let it stay there, d'ye see ;
Tangents and lines we'll leave to the class,
  But the Crescent's the sign for me.
    Chorus.

Life's a college strife,
  Commencement comes full soon !
Let our honors gleam in our Star's bright beam,
  And the rays of our Crescent moon.
    Chorus.

Hand joined in hand,
  And hearts in friendship true,
Under the Crescent and Star we'll stand
  To bid our last adieu.
    Heigh, boys ! raise the strain,
      And let us all agree ;
    Each year shall tighter draw the bonds
      Of Alpha Delta Phi.

HENRY A. POST, Manhattan, 1855.

LII.

TELL US NOT OF FAIRER BOWERS.

Air—" *Cocachelunk.*"

Tell us not of fairer bowers,
　Clad in sweets which sense address;
Not of paths bedecked with flowers—
　Here's the home of happiness!
　　Cocachelunk, etc.

Tell us not of skies enchanting,
　Climes which joys perennial bless,
Groves which fairy sprites are haunting—
　Here's the home of happiness!
　　Cocachelunk, etc.

Alpha Delta! thy bestowing
　Gives our life each joy it hath;
In thy beauty, ever throwing
　Radiance o'er our shaded path!
　　Cocachelunk, etc.

Not the mine's uncounted treasure,
　Not the gold beneath the sea,
Hath a thousandth part the tenure
　That hath bound our hearts to thee.
　　Cocachelunk, etc.

In the life that lies before thee
　May no sorrow e'er befall;
Earth's best gifts be showered o'er thee,
　Heaven's blessings crown them all.
　　Cocachelunk, etc.

Yale, 1855.

5*

LIII.

GOOD LUCK TO ALPHA DELTA.

AIR—"*The King of the Cannibal Islands.*"

Come, brothers, ere we part to-night
We'll do one grateful task aright—
All hail our Star and Crescent bright !
    Good luck to Alpha Delta !

Chorus.

    Then raise the shout as loud as you can,
    Ring out the chorus every man,
    Forever may she lead the van.
        Good luck to Alpha Delta !

For o'er our happy college days
The moon and star shed kindly rays ;
And every day we've cause to praise
    And bless our Alpha Delta !
      Chorus—Then raise the shout, etc.

And ever through the toils of life,
Where care and grief are sadly rife,
There's one release from toil and strife,
    Our dear loved Alpha Delta !
      Chorus—Then raise the shout, etc.

And so, before we part to-night
We'll wish her fortune fair and bright—
Unfading youth, unfailing might !
    GOOD LUCK to Alpha Delta !
      Chorus—Then raise the shout, etc.

                R. S., Manhattan.

LIV.
THE ALUMNI'S RETURN.

AIR—"*Home Again.*"

Once again gathered here
  At our Mother's feet,
The veil of years is fading now,
  The far-off past we greet.
From every land, from every clime,
  With memories we have come,
To take the moss from off thy walls,
  Our Alpha Delta home.

Leaflets fall, rose-tints fade
  In Winter's saddened reign,
But snow-wreaths counterfeiting death,
  Will melt in spring again ;
E'en thus, our love, undimmed by cares,
  Shall never, never die,
But each returning year shall bring
  Our tribute, Delta Phi.

Bound to thee by the ties
  A mother's care has wrought,
Thy harvest home shall see the fruits
  By filial reapers brought;
And if a crown shall grace the brow
  Of Alpha Delta's son,
We lay our chaplet at the feet
  Of her through whom 'twas won.

Gratefully, reverently,
  Round the social board,
We wait a blessing now from thee
  Upon our treasured hoard ;
And when these precious hours are past,
  Our pilgrimage is o'er,
Each devotee will feel new strength
  To face the world once more.

MURRAY DAVIS, Kenyon.

LV.
PARTING SONG.

AIR—"*Good By.*"

Come, brothers, join the farewell song,
  The parting hour draws nigh ;
We to the joys we've loved so long,
  Must bid a last Good By,
  Must bid a last Good By. *Bis.*
    We to the joys, etc.

The shrine that here we've gathered round,
  We'll reverence till we die ;
Our souls are knit, our hearts are bound
  To thee, loved Delta Phi.
  To thee, loved Delta Phi. *Bis.*
    Our souls are knit, etc.

Within these walls, whene'er we meet,
  The hours go swiftly by ;
No joys so wing Time's flying feet,
  As thine, loved Delta Phi,
  As thine, loved Delta Phi. *Bis.*
    No joys so wing, etc.

But they for us have passed away,
  Our last glad hour's flown by,
And we must slowly, sadly say
  A last, a fond Good By,
  A last, a fond Good By. *Bis.*
    And we must slowly, etc.

Then, brothers, join in the farewell song,
  The parting hour draws nigh,
We to the joys we've loved so long,
  Must bid a last Good By,
  Good By, Good By, Good By. *Bis.*
We to the joys we've loved so long,
  Now say Good By, Good By.

C. R. PALMER, Yale, 1855.

LVI.

THERE'S BEAUTY IN YON CRESCENT MOON.

AIR—"*Auld Lang Syne.*"

There's beauty in yon Crescent moon,
  There's beauty in yon Star ;
But unseen beauties symboled there,
  Outshine them both by far.

The mystic tie that binds us here
  Shall bind us till we die ;
And ever will we rally round
  Our Alpha Delta Phi.

D. P. EELS, Hamilton.

LVII.

DOXOLOGY.

Heavenly Father, blessings shower
   On our Alpha Delta Phi,
Let no cloud of discord lower
   Over Alpha Delta Phi ;
Ever may thy power defend us,
   Prosper Alpha Delta Phi ;
Let thy goodness still attend us,
   Bless our Alpha Delta Phi.

C. W. WILDER, Middletown.

LVIII.

DOXOLOGY.

AIR—" *God Save the Queen.*"

Heaven bless thee, Delta Phi !
Heaven save thee, Delta Phi !
   Guard thee for aye ;
Keep thee harmonious,
Happy and glorious,
O'er all victorious,
   Prospered alway.

YALE, 1855.

www.ingramcontent.com/pod-product-compliance
Lightning Source LLC
Chambersburg PA
CBHW021539270326
41930CB00008B/1311